CONNECTING WITH SOURCE

HOW CHANNELING CAN CHANGE YOUR LIFE

BY
OANA MOON

CONNECTING WITH SOURCE
How Channeling can Change your Life by Oana Moon
Published by Dira Publishing Limited
85 Great Portland Street
London
W1W 7LT
United Kingdom

Cover design by Oana Moon

ISBN 978-1-912409-19-8

Dira

I am deeply grateful to all those who contributed to the writing of this book.

☆ ☆ ☆

TABLE OF CONTENTS

1. INTRODUCTION

This work is meant to briefly and clearly explain the concept of Channeling or the Connection with Source for anybody interested in this topic.

It is not a scientific book nor a history of channeling. It is experiential writing based on personal experiences of connecting with Source.

The first part explains channeling from the author's perspective and channeled information, underlining the main truths and false myths about this concept.

Then, the survey results are presented on people who practice channeling to highlight their personal experiences of connecting with Source and the beings of light, the benefits this has brought to their lives, and the main challenges they have faced along the way.

This writing is an invitation to open your heart and mind towards understanding and maybe even experiencing for yourself the magic and joy of connecting with your soul.

Blessings,

Oana Moon

☆ ☆ ☆

2. WHAT IS CHANNELING?

We are all created from the same light of Source (either you call it God, Creator, Divine, Universe, Life Force or any other name), a light that flows through all of us and manifests in unique ways for everyone, depending on what we came to experience and achieve in our lives. This light is always a part of us, no matter where and when we are, what we do, say, think, or what's happening around us. It is always there.

As a permanent part of ourselves, we can always tap into that light by intention. It's like having electricity in our house constantly, but we must push a button to experience the light. It is the same with the light of Source within us. It is always there, waiting to be acknowledged and fully expressed.

In this book I will frequently use the words Source and Divine referring to the same universal, infinite consciousness from where everything was created.

Channeling is about experiencing a direct connection with this Divine inner light and letting it flow freely through us. Therefore, in channeling, we can feel a deep connection with something bigger than us, bigger than what our mind can comprehend. We can feel like we finally found that intangible thing we've always searched for. We can feel like we finally belong, held in an infinite space of love and acceptance.

In channeling, our awareness expands beyond physical limitations, beyond what we've learned and experienced in different environments, and beyond our mind's limitations.

The usual noise of the mind (i.e. thoughts, worries, lists, fears, beliefs, etc.) stops or fades into the background, and **we can clearly distinguish that inner voice that we call intuition**. We can bring that inner wisdom into our everyday life through channeling, letting it guide our major choices and daily endeavours.

☆ ☆ ☆

3. TRUTHS ABOUT CHANNELING

A. WE ARE ALL CHANNELS OF DIVINE LIGHT

Source (or Divine) manifests in various forms through us. Our body is the perfect vessel for our light to be expressed in unique ways.

Our whole body is a channel; we can perceive reality and energies through all our senses and deep inside our bones. Remember that feeling in your gut when you visit a new place or meet a new person. You can feel things deeply inside without any logical explanation or previous knowledge. It's about tapping into that inner knowing that cannot be explained, only lived.

We are all channels, no matter what we do, where we work, what we have learned in school, no matter our age, size, and so on. The same energy of Source flows through as all.

B. CHANNELING IS A STATE OF BEING, A WAY OF LIFE

It is a natural state where we are connected with our most profound selves. Just as it's natural to feel our toes or fingers, our Divine light is a part of us. Staying connected with it is the way to achieving our highest potential in this life, to live life fully aware of the divinity flowing through us and all around us. It helps us enjoy life, embrace all experiences with a childlike curiosity and wonder, and see the beauty of the complex Divine orchestration we are all part of.

This connection brings meaning to our life as we start to understand the importance and lessons beyond our experiences. It helps us feel centred, connected, confident, and in flow with the rhythm of life.

C. EVERY CHANNEL IS UNIQUE

Just like our bodies and personalities are unique, our channels are also. Some of us may be more kinaesthetic, feeling the energies (or shifts in vibration) more clearly in our body, in various forms such as subtle tremors, gut feeling, shivers, buzzing, temperature change, palpitations, etc. The palms, for example, may feel more obviously activated (pulsating) in strong, energetic places or when holding a crystal.

Other people are rather visual. They can see (imagine/visualize) symbols and images that contain explicit or symbolic information.

Some people are more mental. For them, information comes through the mind, as words, phrases, poems, and so on. In the beginning, they need to learn to differentiate better between the logical, everyday mind and their higher mind (connected to the universe's infinite wisdom).

There are people who perceive information through smell, taste (e.g., feeling a certain taste in their mouth), hearing, or touch. For example, I had met people who felt specific perfumes when they connected with various consciousness of light, the smell helping to identify them.

D. OUR CHANNEL IS PERFECTLY ADAPTED TO OUR MISSION IN THIS LIFE

For example, if we are meant to write a book, our channel will be designed to download that specific information at the right moment in the form of words, images, ideas, etc. If we are meant to write poems and inspire others, we can do that fluidly without feeling like forcing anything.

Given that we are all provided with the perfect, most appropriate channel for our life mission, comparing ourselves to others doesn't make sense. **We each have our own rhythm of evolution and expansion.**

For example, in my Level 1 of Dira channeling training, where I first learned how to connect with Source, after three or four days, some people started downloading entire poems in channeling, which seemed so amazing and impossible for me at that time. So, I tried to do the same thing in order to feel as good as them at channeling, and I realized that I was struggling to make rhymes. So, I started laughing as it became clear that it was only my mind making efforts to do something and not a natural flow of information through me. And in time, at my own pace, I have discovered my unique experience of channeling and opened up to what was meant to be expressed through me.

E. THE CHANNEL DEVELOPS THROUGH PRACTICE

It's perfectly natural that in the first days (or weeks) of channeling, we receive maybe only a word, a color, or a sensation in our body. It is OK, and we should be grateful for it because **we always receive what is appropriate for us at that moment in time**.

The more we practice, the more our confidence grows, and the information downloaded expands. This can take weeks, months, or even years. It is important to simply trust our channel and the pace of our journey because it will all make sense in time.

We can channel daily or several times a week. We can ask for guidance or help with specific issues, or simply stay in the energy of Source for a few minutes. We can channel at the beginning of the day or of the week and ask what is important for us to do during that day or week and so on. There is no perfect recipe, as each and every one of us will discover his.

Regarding what we receive in channeling, during my first retreat organized in Glastonbury, for example, one of the participants received a direct initiation from the fairies at the Chalice Well. She started to differentiate vibrations through smell, perceiving different perfumes for specific light beings, completely different from anything she had previously experienced. We all had amazing experiences connecting with the fairies in that retreat, but she was the only one that received that particular activation because it was the most appropriate for her at that moment.

F. FROM THE SPACE OF SOURCE, YOU CAN CONNECT SAFELY WITH EVERYONE AND EVERYTHING

When we connect with Source, we access a space of infinite love and acceptance, a space of oneness where every being is welcome with unconditional love, as it is part of the same Source. Yet, we live in a world of duality where we've learned that things and beings are good and bad and we perceive ourselves as separate from others. Or, from the perspective of Source, there is no separation, no bad or good beings. **Everything and everyone are Divine creations with a Divine purpose**, even if our mind is used to judge and label.

Therefore, from that almighty and encompassing space of Source, we can connect safely with any being, place, object, or aspect of ourselves, with various consciousness, and so on. And in that space, the divinity within us perceives them all with love and compassion, even the beings that have forgotten about the light within them. There is no judgment, differentiation, or separation in that space.

For example, through channeling, I've guided and witnessed young mothers experiencing their first connection and conversations with the child in their womb. They found out what the child needed and how to welcome him/her into this world. Other people were able to meet their light guides, see who they were (e.g., angels, ascended masters, ancestors, etc.), understand how they helped them in their journey, and receive messages from them. On the other hand, in channeling, we can also connect with people or energies that we may fear in physical reality, and what is amazing is that we can see them from the perspective of Source. From that space of unconditional love and acceptance, we can understand more clearly why they are in our lives and their role in our evolution.

G. IN CHANNELING, YOU CAN ACCESS PARALLEL LIVES AND THE INTER-LIFE SPACE

From the space of oneness (Source) accessed through channeling, we can overcome physical limitations and travel in consciousness across time and space. Thus, we can meet our aspects from other lives. We can connect with them, learn from their experiences, and understand how those lives often influence our present emotions and behavior.

Many emotional or mental patterns are reflected in other lives. In channeling we are shown those lives that resonate with us and help us understand and release (transmute) what is no longer beneficial for us now.

For example, a client I've worked with has found that his compulsive eating was caused by having suffered from poverty and lack of food in another life. Many women attracted to spirituality (and channeling) have discovered that their fear of expressing their intuition and unique abilities originates in parallel lives (or past lives, as some call them) where they have been punished (or killed) and accused of sorcery. Many false beliefs such as not being enough, not deserving love, etc., may have been formed in our mother's womb, when we heard our parents fighting about an unwanted pregnancy or worrying about having the resources to care for a baby. We can access, understand and integrate all these memories and patterns with the help of channeling.

☆ ☆ ☆

4. FALSE MYTHS ABOUT CHANNELING

A. CHANNELING IS NOT SCARY

Movies have created a false image of channeling, often confounded with mediumship and scary images of people in a trance. In actuality, there are many ways to connect with other energies and most of us have already intuitively experienced one of these ways. For example, we download messages from our dreams, we have that gut feeling or inner knowing that we call intuition, we talk to God and the saints in our prayers, etc. These are all forms of channeling information from other realms of consciousness.

Some people may feel an affinity for a specific form of channeling, such as connecting with angels, dragons, ascended masters, nature spirits, or the spirits of people who passed away (this is often known as mediumship), etc. It all depends on our mission in this world, as our channel is perfectly adapted to it. Most people called to do that are naturally endowed and further trained to manage those types of encounters and facilitate them for others (the shamans, for example).

Sometimes the ability to connect with other energies manifests naturally from an early age. I've met people who could feel the spirits of those who passed away, and they were scared, resenting their abilities because they made them feel abnormal, and they didn't know what to do with all that. By learning to connect with Source, they've started to understand the meaning of their gift and how to use it to help themselves and others. By connecting from the space of Source, they were no longer afraid of those consciousness forms and they could control when and how to connect with them.

B. IN CHANNELING, YOU DON'T LEND YOUR BODY TO OTHER CONSCIOUS FORMS

We said that there are many forms of channeling, and there is a major difference between channeling from the Source energy and other types. For example, in most channeling protocols, if you want to connect with the consciousness of a tree, you connect directly to that energy. The other possibility, is to connect first with the Source energy and from that infinite library of vibrations, our channel chooses and downloads the energetic imprint of a specific consciousness. Thus, in this case, it is not about lending our body to another consciousness but about downloading an energetic imprint, the most perfectly adapted, safe, and easy to understand for us. This is the specific of the Dira channeling method, which will be later explained.

Channeling from the almighty space of Source brings safety and comfort because we connect with other forms of consciousness from the level of the divinity that flows through all of us. Thus, we don't connect from the level of our ego or personality that might consider itself smaller, weaker, less important than the form of consciousness in front of it, but from the space of the divinity within us, which welcomes any other form of consciousness without judgement, acceptance and love. When we don't connect from that space, we may experience fear, for example, as our limiting beliefs may interfere with the experience.

C. IN CHANNELING, YOU DON'T LOSE CONTROL OF YOUR BODY

The Dira channeling protocol is like a mild form of self-hypnosis where we remain aware of our perceptions and choices. Our mind is like a background observer of everything we experience and we can decide at any moment if we stop or continue to be in that state.

It is true that some channelers are less or completely unaware of what is being expressed through them. It depends on their channeling protocol and their channel's unique features or mission. This is not the case for the channeling protocols where you connect with Source. There, you are completely aware of what is said through your voice, yet, after a while, you might forget a part of what you receive in channeling, so it is useful to record yourself or take notes afterwards.

D. CHANNELING DOES NOT DENY YOUR RELIGIOUS OR

SPIRITUAL BELIEFS AND PRACTICES

There are people from various religions and belief systems that channel. You don't need to renounce your religion or adopt a new one.

However, there is a common basis for channeling with Source: the belief in a greater consciousness that is the origin of everything that is. This belief already exists in most religious and spiritual systems, no matter what we call that source of everything: Creator, Divine, God, Allah, Elohim etc. In channeling, we can connect intentionally with that Source, as we share the same energy. Following the same principle, we can connect with all other creations (conscious forms) from the same Source.

So, **channeling is not a religion. It is only a form of connecting with Source and its various manifestations**.

E. CHANNELING IS NOT FORTUNE-TELLING

This is a very common misunderstanding about channeling. Divine does not intend for us to know everything that will happen in advance because it would deprive us of fully living that experience and the lessons that come with it. Therefore, **we receive in channeling exactly what is appropriate for us to know at that specific moment in time,** so that we can continue to enjoy our lives fully.

Most often, the information comes as advice or guidance from a wiser consciousness who can perceive the unfolding of events beyond the limitations of time and space. So, we may receive some insights about the best way to act in a specific context. The choice is ours to make all the time. From Divine's perspective, all the choices in front of us are good. They all lead to useful experiences and lessons that help us learn and evolve. Therefore, we can ask Divine's guidance about "the best way" to proceed in a certain situation or "the most magnificent possibility" for us at that moment.

F. CHANNELING IS NOT SOMETHING SEPARATE FROM US

We are always connected to the Divine light of Source from where everything was created. That light is a permanent part of us, even if we are not aware of it all the time. This connection to Source doesn't depend on our studies, age, profession, or the number of classes and spiritual training we have attended. It is simply there within, as an internal toolkit meant to guide us in this life. It's only up to us if and when we choose to acknowledge and use it.

What differs is how much we are aware of this inner light in various moments of our life and how well we distinguish this inner voice from other things that go through our mind, such as fears, limiting beliefs, collective patterns, etc. Sometimes we hear this voice clearly, like when we have those spontaneous moments of inspiration where we feel something with our whole being, without any logical argument, and it proves to be right.

The main challenge is to connect with our intuition intentionally and clearly, as most of us cannot control those brief moments of inspiration. Or we can discover and explore various ways to connect, such as meditation, drawing, dancing, or different channeling protocols.

G. CHANNELING IS NOT A BUSINESS, IT IS A SOUL CALLING

Channeling is a deep calling of our soul. Some see it as a tool to make money, but it in actuality, it helps us raise our vibration and consequently, attract more abundance and opportunities in our lives. It helps to uncover our unique talents and abilities, guiding us towards the perfect context of using them for our benefit and others'. Following this inner calling opens the doors to new possibilities, fulfilment, and transformation.

H. ONLY VERY SPECIAL AND PURE PERSONS CAN CONNECT WITH SOURCE

This is another false myth that will be clarified in the following section.

☆ ☆ ☆

5. WHO CAN CHANNEL?

A. EVERYBODY CAN CONNECT DIRECTLY WITH SOURCE

Everybody can connect with Source because we are all manifestations of the same Divine light. And happily, we no longer need intermediaries for this (i.e., priests, gurus, masters, seers, etc.). We are all good enough to connect ourselves. It is only a matter of believing in our inner light.

B. WE ARE ALL AND ALWAYS CONNECTED WITH SOURCE

It doesn't matter our profession, age, religion, or how much training we did. That connection is always there, beyond the physical experiences and limitations. However, the way we perceive it, how clearly and how much we trust it differ from person to person.

Some people believe in this connection, calling it in various ways such as intuition, inner voice, gut feeling etc. Others choose to reject it and trust what society has taught them. Since young kids, we were told to believe in what we see, touch, and understand with our logical minds. We were taught not to believe in magic and fairy tales because we'd be considered crazy and isolated. We were taught that we were too small, too unworthy to be able to talk to God, and so on. Our light is covered by many such beliefs inherited from our family, church, society, etc.

☆ ☆ ☆

6. HOW DO WE CHANNEL?

A. INTUITIVE CHANNELING

There are different ways to connect with that Divine part of our-selves. As it has always been inside us, some of us have been connecting with it intuitively through dreams, premonitions, or thoughts that came out of nowhere, with no explanation or logical arguments backing them, but that proved right when we followed them.

Artists usually connect with this higher source of knowledge when they create masterpieces that move us deeply and remain pow-erful over time. Great inventors like Tesla also downloaded in-formation by connecting intuitively to a universal pool of wisdom beyond the experiences and information acquired in physical re-ality. This way, major inventions were downloaded, changing the course of humanity. Likewise, listening to our intuition can deeply change our lives.

B. INTENTIONAL CHANNELING

Some of us may channel intuitively, but this type of connection cannot usually be controlled. It only comes naturally in specific moments and circumstances, and some have tried to identify and reproduce the specific context in which that connection was es-tablished: certain music, being in nature, dancing, or performing certain rituals, for example.

Rituals and intermediaries. Rituals have been used by religious figures, shamans, mediums, witches, etc. as a way to connect with Divine and other conscious forms. They usually involve an interface between us and the divinity: a person (the shaman, the witch, the seer) who connects with other consciousness and transmits the messages, as well as certain objects, plants, sub-stances or drugs, movements, words or songs meant to facilitate that connection. Most often, this connection is only with an aspect of Source: a specific god/goddess, ancestors, nature spirits, etc. Therefore, this way may sometimes maintain a feeling of being separate, unable, or even unworthy of connecting directly with Source.

Direct channeling. The strongest and most empowering way to connect with Source is through direct channeling, by tapping into that Divine light within us. We can do that through various proto-cols. Some methods are meant to connect with conscious forms such as angels, dragons, ascended masters, nature spirits, etc. Others, such as the Dira protocol, are meant to help us connect directly with Source, and from there, with other consciousness as well.

In the end, *it doesn't even matter how. What matters is to connect on our own and to feel the Divine light flowing through us, to let it express freely in our life so that we can tap into our highest potential*. But as we've said before, we need to believe in ourselves as the creation and manifestation of the Divine.

C. EXAMPLES OF PROTOCOLS FOR CONNECTING WITH SOURCE AND THE LIGHT BEINGS

The Dira protocol was initiated by Lubna Kharusi, the founder of the Dira International. This protocol teaches us to connect with Source (usually named Divine), that infinite space from which we can access any consciousness, such as our higher self, angels, ascended masters, etc. The basic principle of the protocol is Oneness, meaning that everything is interconnected and Divinely orchestrated for a beautiful purpose. The only prerequisite for channeling the light of Source is acknowledging and believing in a Supreme Source of everything.

The Dira Journey includes 7 channeling practice levels, lasting from 9 days (Level 1) to 1 year of daily practice (Level 7). I started using the Dira protocol in March 2020, and it has completely transformed and enriched my spiritual journey and everyday life. You can find out more about Dira International at

www.dirainternational.com.

GAPI is an intuitive channeling method meant to facilitate a connection with high vibration consciousness such as angels, dragons, ascended masters, etc. The name comes from the four stages of this method: Grounding, Alignment, Protection, and Invocation. It is promoted and taught by Ramona Popescu, in her the spirituality classes. GAPI was my first introduction to channeling.

Some **energy healing methods** facilitate a temporary connection with Source, where you can connect with the same universal consciousness of source (but without naming it Source, allowing each person to label it through their own experience). This connection happens by going down through several layers of emotions or beliefs.

There are many channeling methods and everyone will find the most appropriate for them and their life journey. With time, we may even find our unique method of connecting, based on everything we've learned and experienced.

☆ ☆ ☆

7. CONNECTING WITH SOURCE

A. FIRST EXPERIENCES OF CHANNELING

The first connection with Source is usually about experiencing what we are usually taught to believe as impossible. It opens the doors to a completely **new world** and to a **new way** of perceiving ourselves:

Adriana from Italy describes it as "an unexpected experience. I was a little afraid I couldn't do it like others, but the magic happened, and the invisible world opened in all its splendor, in images and colors."

"The first time I entered into channeling, it felt like I actually discovered America. It felt like it was everything I needed to feel at that moment, as well as lots of gratitude." (Irina, Romania)

People often describe their first connection with Source as: "exaltation" and "inner change," "a feeling of complete expansion" (Razvan, Romania), or "oneness and non judgement" (Sinziana, Romania).

It may be a very emotional experience, so people often cry when they first reach that state of **profound communion and peace**. In those moments, we can deeply experience a direct connection with Source and the whole creation, beyond the separation and contrast from the physical reality.

"The first time, it was magic. It was with tears and release. I dissolved into the light of Source. It was incredible the way I felt. I felt peace, at peace with myself, and I felt we were all one." (Nicoleta, Romania)

For many, this first connection feels like finally being whole and like a long-awaited "**Homecoming**". The soul recognizes the energy of Source as home.

"After my first experience, I felt like I arrived home. I was safe, good, and exactly when and where I was supposed to be. I felt full of love, peace, and clarity, and any lack of self-confidence disappeared. I was still myself but stronger, safer, and whole" (Adriana, Romania)

Even from the first connection, we can experience the presence of Source and find **answers to our questions**. These answers are usually felt as true in our whole body and being, beyond the doubts of our mind:

"In my first experience of channeling, I felt without a doubt that the answer came from Source because it was soft but firm, and it showed me where I was lying to myself and didn't want to see the truth. I received the most authentic answers even if I didn't like them." (Mihaela, Romania)

B. THE EXPERIENCE OF SOURCE

As mentioned before, every person experiences Source in their own unique way, depending on their channel features and their life journey. And from the first connection, every person has a specific way of knowing that they are channeling (even if that way may change in time).

i. Visual signals

For example, many people see a strong light (usually white) when they experience the connection. The Source is usually associated with **white light**, which includes all the other light spectrum, just like Source consists of everything that is, all the vibrations in existence.

ii. Energy

The white light is often experienced in association with a very expansive energy, like an **infinite ocean of light, love, peace, gratitude**, and other wonderful feeling.

"For me, this feeling is of infinite love… full of gratitude towards humans and unparalleled wisdom, clarity. I feel overwhelmed with gratitude and love towards the Divine Supreme!" (Suchitra, Oman).

In the space of Source, we can finally experience a deep **connection with everything that is** (or what is called oneness). Alya, from Oman, describes this connection as "expansion, one with all, Divine love radiating through my being."

Sometimes, the connection may be recognized or accompanied by a more or less strong **activation of our chakras**. We may feel a subtle vibration, warming, or tingling, especially in the heart and crown chakras, representing the centre of our being and the connection point with Source. For example, I recognize the connection through a subtle activation of my heart, followed by a tingling energy rising along my spine. Others feel stronger their higher chakras: "I feel an activation of my 6th and 7th chakras, with tingling, and my whole body relaxes." (Cristina C., Romania)

iii. Body sensations

For some people, the experience of Source may be **deeply physical**:

"I feel a very strong vibration, sounds in my ears, pressure in my head, a warming sensation and big joy (sometimes so big I break into tears)," says Corina P. from Romania.

In many cases (mine included), the physical experiences may come with time, and this happens for different reasons: we may be less connected with our body and this connection comes back gradually, or we need to trust first in the intangible before it reveals itself more physically, etc.

iv. Inner voice

For many people, the connection is announced by an inner voice, which we usually call our intuition voice.

In this case, there is a specific **welcoming phrase** that we may say once we are in channel, such as: "Hello, we are glad to meet you again" (Irina, from the United Kingdom), "We are here" (Cristina, from Romania, Alexandra from Spain, my case and others), "What is your question?" (Lubna, Oman), etc. This is like a signal to the mind that we are in a channeling.

v. Our experience of Source evolves over time.

This connection is a very deep, personal, and evolving journey on its own. It evolves with us like a river that changes its features (e.g., length, depth, or speed).Depending on our life journey and ourselves in that specific period (i.e., our personality and needs). So, in every moment of our life, our connection with Source evolves, perfectly adapted to who we are then and there. If, in the beginning, we may need to do the whole protocol carefully, paying attention to each step, with time, the connection may become instant, or sometimes we may simply find ourselves in channel, because we have finally come to embody that connection as a permanent part of us.

☆ ☆ ☆

8. CHANNELING SURVEY

In February-March 2023, I surveyed 134 people who have practised channeling for different periods of time and with different channeling protocols. The following section presents the results of this survey.

The survey sample

Most of the subjects (68%) were from Romania (as they were easier for me to find), followed by Oman (where the Dira community was founded) with 10%, the United Kingdom (3%), Germany (3%), Spain (2%), by Denmark, Switzerland, Italy and Netherlands (each with 1.5 %), as well as Mauritius, Saudi Arabia, Turkey, EAU, USA or Austria, with 1 person each.

Women strongly dominate the sample (91%), which is a common occurrence for many spiritual courses, retreats, and events.

The age categories best represented are those between 35 and 54 years old (68%), but also with a good share of people over 54 years (12.7%). The increasing interest among younger people towards spirituality and self-development is visible in the strong share of the categories under 34 years old (19%).

The experience of channeling varies from one month to 30 years. Some consider that this connection has manifested intuitively from childhood or younger age and only later consciously, by following a specific protocol.

The practice frequency varies. About 97 % of the people who answered channel at least once a week. Those who practice almost daily dominate (47%), followed by those who channel 1-2 times/week (25%), 3-5 times/week (13%) or whenever needed (6.3%). For 2.4%, channeling feels like a way of living, like they are always connected to Source. Andreea A., from Romania, connects "daily, whenever I don't have clarity or feel connected to my essence."

A. CHANNELING METHOD

There is no blanket rule about our channeling practice. **We can channel whenever we feel like. Yet, the more we do it, the more we feel our channel and clarity expanding**.

> With 69% of the answers, meditation is the most frequently used method to connect with Source and other forms of consciousness

Meditation remains one of the most popular ways to introduce people to spirituality and connect with non-physical realms. However, the majority (85%) use at least two methods of channeling.

CHANNELING METHODS

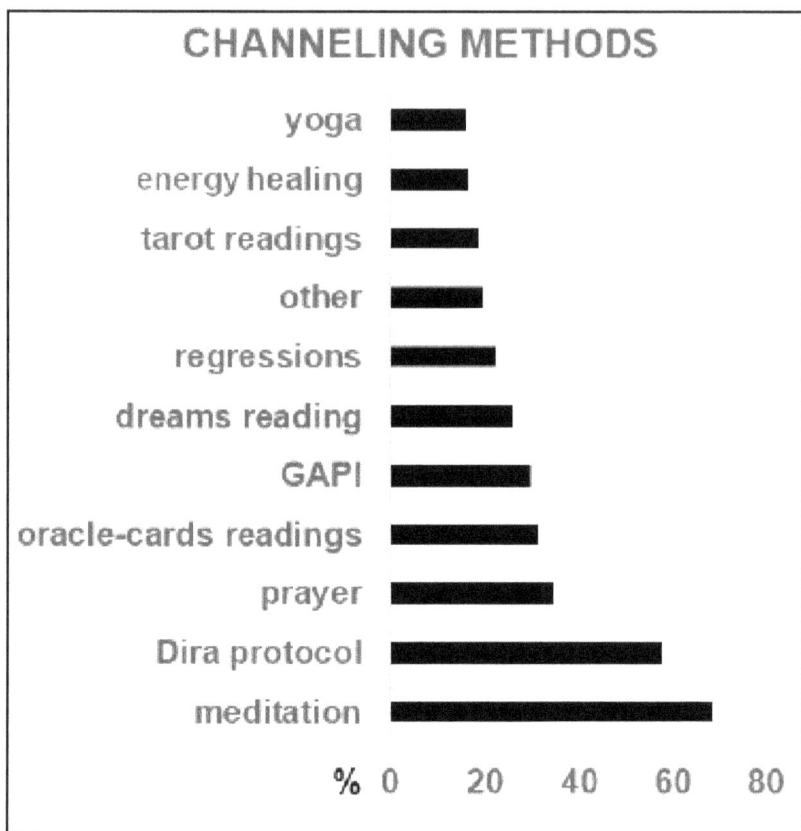

Method	%
yoga	
energy healing	
tarot readings	
other	
regressions	
dreams reading	
GAPI	
oracle-cards readings	
prayer	
Dira protocol	
meditation	

As most of the sample was found in two main channeling communities, the results highlight the methods taught in these communities: the **Dira protocol** (56%) and the GAPI meditation (30%). **Prayer** also has a significant share (34%), indicating the impact of our religious practice. Other connection techniques such as oracle-cards readings (31%), dreams interpretation (26%), regression (22%), tarot readings (18%), theta healing (16%), yoga (16%) are often linked to specific therapies and activities that integrate channeling. People usually mix several methods, depending on each context (i.e., inspiration, personal needs, their client's needs, etc).

B. LIFE BEOFRE CHANNELING

When questioned about the state of their life before learning how to channel, about 65% of the answers mentioned the search for **a (deeper) meaning of life**, the need to understand themselves and the sense of their existence beyond the ordinary social and physical environment (i.e., job, family, various social roles, etc.).

About 65 % of people searched for a deeper meaning of life before discovering channeling

More than 40% of the people said they were caught up in many **worries and thoughts or felt somehow blocked**, and over 1/3 of the sample talked about **feeling disconnected, lost, confused, or not loving and appreciating themselves.** These topics are increasingly frequent nowadays, pushing people to search for a higher purpose, connection, fulfilment, and inner peace.

More than 40% of the people said they were caught up in many **worries** and thoughts or felt somehow blocked, and over 1/3 of the sample talked about feeling disconnected, lost, confused, or not loving and appreciating themselves. These topics are increasingly frequent nowadays, pushing people to search for a higher purpose, connection, fulfilment, and inner peace.

Over 20% of the answers indicated the weight of **stress** and agitation (27 %), a difficult relationship with their own body (23%), as well as the struggle with fears and phobias (22%).

HOW WAS YOUR LIFE BEFORE LEARNING HOW TO CHANNEL?

I had physical health issues

I was searching for a partner

I had financial difficulties

I was in a job that I didn't identify with anymore

I had a difficult relationship with my partner

Other situations

I had difficulties in managing my emotions

I had a difficult relationship with my family

I was caught up in my fears/phobias

I had a difficult relationship with my body

I was stressed, agitated

I didn't love/appreciated myself

I felt disconnected, lost, confused

I felt blocked, limited somehow

I had lots of worries, thoughts

I was searching for a (deeper) meaning of life

% 0   20   40   60

Between 10 and 20% of the sample mentioned other situations such as a problematic relationship with their family (18%) or partner (16%), difficulties in managing and understanding their emotions (17%), being in a job that they didn't identify with anymore (12%), financial difficulties (poor or unstable revenues) (11%) or searching for a partner (11%).

Fewer mentioned physical health issues (8%) or depression and panic attacks (5%).

C. LIFE AFTER CHANNELING

Regarding how people's lives have improved after learning to channel, 76% of the answers mentioned their **trust in divinity and Divine guidance**.

> About 76% of the answers highlighted an increasing or new-found trust in divinity and divine guidance as the main benefits of channeling

WHAT ASPECTS OF YOUR LIFE HAVE IMPROVED AFTER YOU STARTED TO CHANNEL

Other
New house
Less depression/anxiety
Better income
New job
Improved physical health
Relationship with my partner
New fulfilling activities
Self-expression
Family relationships
Relationship with my body
Better choices
New opportunities
New abilities/passions
New people
More freedom
Self-confidence
Releasing patterns
Expanded awareness
Enjoying life
More meaning to life
Feeling connected
Selflove
Feeling calmer
Trusting Source/guidance

% 0 20 40 60 80

Also, more than 50% of the answers were about:

- Finding more peace (65%),

- Increasing self-love and self-acceptance (63%),

- Feeling connected (60%),

- Finding more meaning in life (55%),

- Enjoying life (52%).

Other frequent benefits of opening to channeling are self-confidence (47%), freedom (40%), meeting new people (40%), discovering new abilities and passions (39%), finding new/more opportunities in life (38%), making better (more conscious) choices (38%), improved relationship with their own body (34%) or family (34%), self-expression (34%), finding fulfilling activities (27%), improved relationships with their partner (26%), improved physical health (25%), with 18% overcoming depression and panic attacks. Some have higher (more stable) incomes (22%) and others have changed their jobs (23%) or houses (13%).

☆ ☆ ☆

9. BENEFITS OF CHANNELING

A. TRUSTING SOURCE (DIVINE), TRUSTING LIFE AND THE DIVINE GUIDANCE

One of the most important changes that channeling brings to our lives is the increasing trust in Divine: i.e., in Divine's guidance, support, protection, and unconditional love. This also reinforces our trust that everything is part of a Divine orchestration, and our soul knows exactly where our place is and the right steps towards it.

Corina C. (Romania) says: "I always feel protected, more relaxed, and I lovingly trust the Divine plan. I enjoy everything that happens to me, and I appreciate a lot more life, people, events, and emotions."

"I trust in the 'unknown' Divine," says Roxana from Denmark.

"I have learned to trust myself more, to trust my intuition. To trust Divine that they guide us on the right path." (Mihaela, Romania)

Trust helps people **accept things as they come** and understand the Divine orchestration behind them. "I accept easier everything that I experience (i.e., daily challenges), and I try to see the lesson behind that experience. I trust Divine!" (A.C.)

Channeling opens the door to a **new relationship with life and the Divine, to letting go of control** and simply enjoying things as they come:

"I have more trust in Divine and in the fact that whatever happens is appropriate. I don't make plans as often as before because I want to control everything in our lives. I let myself be guided more often." (Cozmina, Romania)

"Even if in my everyday life I experience losses in my relationships, and even if I am not fully content about my job when I connect with Divine, I feel an inexplicable but pleasant state of joy, safety, and trust. I feel like everything will be OK, and even if it is not how I want, I let Divine orchestrate things in their natural way. Then, the fight, stress, and sorrow disappear, and acceptance comes following the trust in Divine. I am delighted that I can finally let go of control. It is Divine to be able to do that and feel" (Adriana M., Romania).

The relationship with God changes entirely after channeling, from fear and separation (from seeing God as a powerful and frightening presence living somewhere in the sky) to love, trust, and a permanent connection.

"Before channeling, I had a fear-based relationship with God. After channeling, my relationship with God is Love." (K.S., Oman)

"The biggest transformation for me is that I no longer feel separated from Divine. I know that I'm always supported and guided by Divine, by angels and beings of light." (Ana Cristina, Denmark)

Feeling loved by Divine is another major aspect that comes with the experience of channeling. This highlights the dismantling of the old image of a severe, punishing God, replacing it with a representation of unconditional love, acceptance, and guidance.

 "The most important experience was the feeling of being loved exactly as I am and no matter what I do." (Maria Cristina, Romania).

"I am always connected, guided, loved by God! I feel God in everything that I do and experience!" (Robert, Romania)

This new perspective on Divine is expected because, in channeling, most of Divine's messages are about their love for humanity, a constant reminder of the love that creates and permeates everything. For example, in my case every time I enter into channeling, whenever I ask what I am supposed to know, first comes the reminder that I am loved.

B. FINDING PEACE

Many people (65%) mentioned **finding peace** as an effect of channeling:

"I found peace, harmony, and balance. Somehow, I see and feel things more in-depth. I have more clarity, I am calmer, and I've learned to act first and think later, but to follow my intuition and my soul" (Aurora, Romania)

It is true that through channeling, we can **find the acceptance and strength to go through the most difficult challenges** and find peace even in the middle of the strongest storms:

"I would share that the unexpected is possible! That you can be going through the most awful time in your life and channeling can give you moments of calm." (S.O., Canada)

C. SELF-LOVE AND SELF-ACCEPTANCE

Self-love and self-acceptance are mentioned by most people (63%) as part of an improving relationship with themselves. For example, the most important channeling experience for Sinziana (Romania) was: "the improvement of the relationship with myself, as well as the release of judgments and criticism towards myself."

"My life has transformed radically since I started channeling in so many ways that it's hard to formulate a one-page answer. First, I've learned to love myself more and be patient with my growth process. I quit smoking, and my life has been way more balanced," says Calin, from Romania.

Self-development and self-discovery are important steps on the journey towards self-acceptance and love. Channeling can bring inner transformation, more presence, and more self-awareness in our lives.

"I feel that I still am in a process of transformation and growth. The most liberating transformation is the fact that I am present. I enjoy more what I am and what's around me. First, I feel and accept myself exactly as I am, and I feel and accept also the people around me as they are. I've started living, not only existing like a small robot." (Oana, United Kingdom).

D. FEELING CONNECTED

Since feeling lost, confused, and disconnected are frequent symptoms in our present society, channeling supports and emphasizes **a permanent, safe connection to a supreme Divine power**. Hence, this is mentioned as one of the strongest life-changing experiences in many answers.

"I know that no matter what I go through and how difficult an event in my life would appear, I am not alone. God is with me always," says Ana P. from Romania.

"When I acknowledged the presence of Divine in every particle of me, I feel the highest joy. Every time I enter into channeling, I feel more aware of myself and of my wonderful connection with this world" (Andreea T., Romania)

For some people, this connection has been felt since very early times, even **since childhood**, but it was consciously established later when they learned a specific method of connecting to the Divine: "Practically, my connection with Divinity has been forever, but consciously only from 2017" (Carmen, Switzerland).

This is why the first experience of channeling may often feel like a **homecoming**: "The first time I felt the pure connection with my Inner divinity, it was like coming back Home," says Maria Magdalena from Romania.

A frequent difference from previous intuitive channeling

experiences is **feeling stronger the connection with Divine**. This appears to be common feedback after making the first connection with Source through a channeling protocol.

"The connection with Divine was at another level, more profound. It is a state that you reach, and your soul wants to stay there longer. It opened a small door towards Divine that I didn't experience before" (Rodica, Romania)

This Divine connection may slowly become a major part of our lives, enabling us to explore and understand our inner and outer worlds, past, present, and future. For example, Andreea A. from Romania affirms that "this is my way to travel in my inner world and to gain clarity, to open spaces within me. This connection is vital for me."

E. FINDING MORE MEANING IN LIFE AND THE LIFE MISSION

In channeling, people **find answers to many life-related questions**, helping them to understand why things happen and the higher meaning behind different experiences.

"Channeling has given me a new perspective on what life is really about, and it has brought so much more meaning and answers." (Mariana, USA)

For many people, channeling helps them make more sense of their life and **find their purpose or vocation**.

"I discovered my vocation. And every day is a conscious way to follow my path." Says Anca T., from Romania.

"I found my life mission – that soul calling, in astrology and the possibility to work with other people for their evolution and personal development." (Luminita, Romania)

"I've understood what my life purpose was, and more opportunities to fulfil it are coming my way. Everything comes with ease in my life." (Bianca, Romania)

Finding the life mission helps us to better **navigate life, to find our path or place in this world, and learn to surrender to the universal flow**.

"I found my life mission, and I've learned to truly love myself, which propelled me on my way of healing and evolution. Now I can give more pure love and help others on their own journey to healing. I've also learned to release the constant impulse to control everything. I've learned to surrender to the universe and co-create with it. This has brought me more peace, synchronicity, and easiness in life" (Denise, Germany).

Note. Finding out the life mission is one of people's main quests and one of the most frequent questions in channeling sessions.

There is a common belief that we all come into this life with one big mission to achieve, but the truth is more nuanced. Our life is not about only one big activity or mission. Or, if we want to see it like that, our big general mission here is to be in our light, to re-discover the Divine light that flows through us and let it be expressed freely, let it guide us.

A life mission does not imply that we are supposed to do only one big thing or activity in our life. We can be in our light in various ways and contexts over the years and do more things aligned with the Divine light that manifests through us. So, talking about only one activity as a life mission is often our mind's way to simplify and put a label on us and our life. Or, we are more than a label. We are more than one-lifetime activity, we are so much more. Therefore, if our life mission, for example, is to inspire and guide people to find their inner light, this may happen in various forms, such as guiding and supporting our family, being a teacher who supports his students, writing a book, or having public lectures and classes, etc. All these activities are important for our and others' evolution, as each will uncover an aspect of our divinity.

Our life mission does not have to be something grandiose. Many people expect their life mission to be something huge and public for all humanity, but our contribution can happen in subtler and unexpected ways. It doesn't have to be something glorious or laborious. We tend to underestimate our contribution to this world. For example, being an anchor of peace and love for our family and friends is no less important than speaking to the masses. We all do our work and impact in ways that our mind cannot fully comprehend but make all the sense from a higher perspective.

Furthermore, the Creator within us always generates many possibilities for us to shine in our light and fulfil our mission in this world. So, we are always on the right path. And when it's about choosing the most magnificent possibilities for us, the guidance is always inside, in our body, in the ease or discomfort, the joy or tension that our body experiences at that moment.

In conclusion, **we can be and do many things, but the thing that connects all these puzzle pieces is being in our light, knowing it, and letting it shine freely.**

F. ENJOYING LIFE

A major transformation brought by one's connection with their soul is letting ourselves enjoy life, finding happiness and seeing blessings in the small things.

"The biggest transformation is within me. Everything that I experience now is different from what I did until now. I didn't allow myself to enjoy life, and I was living always limiting myself," says Denisa, from Romania.

Our perspective of life changes when we start seeing it without the layers of conditioning.

"I started enjoying everything that I have. Before, I couldn't see that my life was full of great things, things that I forgot to love.

Now I have hope, and I always feel protected. I love life." (Iris, Romania)

G. SELF-CONFIDENCE AND SELF-EXPRESSION

Increasing self-confidence is a very common effect of learning how to channel and connect with the infinite wisdom that has always been within us. Every day and every time we follow that inner guidance and see where it leads us, it increases our confidence in ourselves, our abilities, and our connection with Source.

"The deepest realization that I had was the full confidence in myself" (Manuela P., Romania)

"Channeling helped me to have more trust in myself and in what I do. It enabled me to connect more with myself. "(Robert, Romania)

"I feel like I can deal with anything. I'm confident that there is a solution for everything." (Zulfa, Oman)

"I trust myself and life more. I trust that I am ready and supported even when I face challenges that my mind would consider impossible to overcome." (Alexandra P., Romania)

"I gained more confidence in what I receive as messages, guidance, images, and intuition in my everyday life. I see how everything is interconnected, and I make easier connections between different moments of my life, between what I perceive, the filters through which I see things, and the way things manifest in the physical world. I've learned to ask frequently what I feel, what feels right to do, and how beneficial one action is for me and others before making a decision. At the same time, I now understand that what I receive as messages or inner guidance can take a different form in the physical realm, or the manifestation time may be longer than I initially perceived. I think I've gained more flexibility in accepting what comes up beyond my expectations." (Mihaela O., Romania)

Sometimes, channeling comes to **validate what we've already known internally**, but we haven't known if and how to trust those feelings: "With channeling, I have received many confirmations regarding my spiritual evolution directly from Source," says Valentina, from Romania.

Channeling is a way to build self-empowerment, which represents a major step in our personal development. By directly connecting with Source, we can acknowledge our divinity, letting go of old beliefs and patterns where we gave away our power to various people and authorities. We don't need some guru or master to tell us what is good for us because we can feel and know the truth for ourselves. **The most appropriate answers come through our own channel.**

"The most important revelation for me was the confirmation that we don't need intermediaries to connect with the higher realms. Even if I had situations where I was thus "guided" by others, I tended to believe that my ego was thinking that. I believed we were not special/ powerful/ pure enough to connect with the ascended masters or angels by ourselves. Somehow, this program or religious belief was dismantled." (Monica, Romania)

Self-confidence helps us make better choices for ourselves and, most importantly, be aware of and express our inner light. **Self-confidence helps us to speak our truth and be our true selves**, letting go of society's roles and expectations.

"I have gained confidence in myself, confidence in speaking my truth" (Anarouby, Mauritius)

"I became more alive and self-aware. And able to be true to myself and make the necessary decisions and choices aligned with who I truly am. I healed so many relationships in my life, most importantly my relationship with myself." (Asaad, United Kingdom)

"I learned to commit to myself to show up in greater ways every day, to speak my truth, and to live and express myself more authentically. I am practising focusing my energy on the physical world and developing a business that generates a lifestyle of security, abundance, and exploration for myself and my family. I am proud that I stand up, vulnerable, and transparent with nothing to hide. I take pride that I am learning to be fully present & learning to connect to people with true empathy. And that I am learning to transcend old patterns." (Ozzy, Dubai)

Note. Such revelations are normal in the present energetic context, where we experience a so-called **R-Evolution (Revelation + Evolution)**, meaning that our true essence, the golden light within our hearts, comes up to the surface, cleansing our layers, our shadows, and burdens, all our masks. This is the time for **the Revelation of our true selves and Evolution towards embodying them**. This is actually the higher meaning of our life, the true direction, besides the temporary, individual objectives that we assume along the way. The purpose is to be what we truly are, to go through a chrysalid's process and become the butterfly that flies free. And we can fly free, like the butterflies on a sunny meadow, caressed by the sunlight. That butterfly is in our belly – the true self coming out of the chrysalid, and we can feel its wings fluttering. We can feel it in our bellies, hearts, and bodies, like a calling or preparation for something big.

True self-confidence is not built in comparison with others. It is not fair to compare ourselves to others, as each one's light is unique. Where we have less, somebody else has more, and this only makes us all perfect pieces of a larger, infinite Divine puzzle. This is natural because we are all having our unique paths. And our unique paths are perfectly interlaced in the greater puzzle, thus creating a permanently evolving path at the collective (and creation) level. This path changes with us every minute and second, and this is beautiful to witness. So, **feeling small(er) than others is an illusion because we are all great and infinite, only in different ways**!

H. FREEDOM AND RELEASE OF OLD CONDITIONING

Experiencing freedom is a popular benefit of connecting with Divine and the beings of light, and it is mentioned by 40 % of the survey participants. They mostly refer to the freedom to speak their truth and live authentically.

"I feel that I've regained my freedom, and now I can offer it to others as well, without expectations," says Oana N, from Romania.

Freedom usually comes with the process of **shedding old layers of limitations and conditioning.** We are born with many of these, and also accumulate them with life experience. But they all have a common purpose: to unveil, step by step, our inner light, the unique aspects of our divinity. This de-layering process is progressive, in the most appropriate way and rhythm for everyone. It can't be rushed or postponed because it only unfolds when the soul is completely ready to release that layer. The release can be emotional, mental, or physical.

"I've understood why I experience certain blockages and that they are created only by my mind. Once acknowledged, they don't have much power anymore, and you can simply start discovering new perspectives. Even more, life starts to make more sense. You understand who you are and your purpose," says Andreea from the Netherlands.

"I am better at letting go of difficult emotions. In the past, I would hold on to the emotion for weeks, and it would affect my lifestyle and relationships." (LM, Oman)

"I felt how my mental blocks were melting one by one with each session. After one of the first sessions of channeling, the name of my business came to me." (Lavinia, Germany)

i. MEETING NEW PEOPLE AND FINDING NEW OPPORTUNITIES IN LIFE

Meeting new people and finding new opportunities are frequently mentioned among the benefits of channeling (40 % and 38 % of the answers). The rise of our vibration through channeling contributes to reshaping our physical reality. Thus, we start to attract new people, events, and things in our lives.

"I've started to better understand what was going on around me. There were new people that appeared around me, needing my help." (Corina C, Romania)

C.M. from Romania talks about profound inner and outer changes: "Working every day with myself, everything around me has changed and started to reflect my new inner harmony."

Inner transformations may be reflected outside as **new job opportunities (23%) or new houses (13%)**. **It may also deeply transform our relationships.**

"Through Divine guidance, I changed twice the country I lived in, and another journey follows, for a longer period, also coming through Divine guidance. It's not the relationships that changed, but my perception of those relationships. This changed a lot of those connections." (Lora, Republic of Moldova)

J. SELF-DEVELOPMENT

Self-knowledge is one of the most important benefits of channeling. By connecting with our soul, we can understand ourselves better. We can understand our emotions, thoughts, and behavioral patterns and really find out what our soul needs beyond social conditioning.

For Maria Tatiana (Romania), channeling has brought "expansion, growth and transformation," while for Roxana (Romania), it helped her to "discover herself".

"I have chewed on my fingernails for 30 years and discovered and released the cause in one channeling session. I understood that it was an anxiety inherited from my mother. I let go of my need for control, and I learnt to put myself first. And many others… I consider channeling one of the greatest blessings in my life." (Ioana, Romania)

Hrug from the United States, for example, mentions: "the ability to connect with me, in a less cerebral, more visceral intuitive way."

Enhanced focus also appears frequently in people's answers:

"Channeling helps me in my mental self-control and to focus on what I need to do at the moment. It opened me to be thankful every moment for what I am and what I have." (Cristian, Romania)

Sometimes, channeling may help us enrich, develop, or do our job better. We can bring Divine guidance and our unique imprint into our careers through channeling. For example, if we are meant to work with other people (i.e., teachers, coaches, sales, public relations, etc.), channeling will help us find our magic and tune in better to our client's state of mind and needs. It may bring a higher vibration (of love, wisdom, or peace) into our interactions. If you are a therapist, channeling may help you better connect with the people in front of you and hold their space so they can freely express their deepest emotions and wounds. Thus, you can hold a space of safety and unconditional acceptance where they can open up fully. You can tune in to their deepest needs and address them appropriately at that moment in time. And this occurs naturally if you put the intention to open up to Divine guidance, to what's best for you and your clients.

"When I work with people in therapies, before they come, I receive information that will help me and help them, sometimes even modalities to work with them," says Corina P., a hypnotherapist from Romania.

K. MAKING BETTER, MORE CONSCIOUS CHOICES

Every day we are in an ocean of opinions, words, beliefs, values, expectations, and projections, ours and others. They surround us the minute we turn on our TV, laptop, or phone, when we start talking to our family, friends, or colleagues. So, how do we choose among all these possibilities?

Making better (best) choices for ourselves is another self-development (and self-empowering) aspect enhanced by channeling. From the infinite opportunities in front of us, we can find out which is the most appropriate for us at that moment, the most aligned to our highest good, by simply asking for guidance.

"Channeling helped me make quick and accurate decisions with no regrets. Generally, my life is better and more fulfilling, and I understand my purpose, and doors that were not there earlier have opened up for me," says S.J. from Oman.

"I feel what I need to do. I feel what is the best for me. I make the best decisions." (Georgiana, Romania)

Gaining clarity from the guidance received in channeling is a major factor that leads us to better choices:

"Channeling gave me clarity in everything I chose to do and confidence in my choices" (Florina, Romania)

L. IMPROVED RELATIONSHIPS

About 34% of the survey respondents mentioned improved relationships with their family or partner (26%).

In channeling, we can find the clarity, peace, and compassion to reassess and reshape our perspective on relationships. Thus, inner changes may be mirrored outside in **new ways of seeing**

and interacting with our loved ones.

"I simply found myself, and I found joy in simple things. I found appreciation for myself and those around me and the trust that everything that comes is for my highest good. I was on the verge of divorce, and now I have a very fulfilling relationship with my husband." (Ioana, Romania)

Some people have even **found their partner** after starting to channel and connect with their intuition.

"I feel like talking about an essential moment in my life that completely changed the course of my existence from that moment onwards. I met my husband in a workshop about intention, and even if my body initially rejected him, afterwards, during an exercise with my eyes closed, I received an image where I was going into his arms. Something within me that initially rejected the idea wanted to turn around and leave the room, but I consciously overcame my initial resistance and followed the guidance. An entire journey of self-knowledge, deconstruction, and reconstruction has followed on multiple planes, as neither of us could have imagined. The path continues... In time, I understood that what I felt in my body at that moment was both resistance and guidance." (Mihaela O., Romania)

M. IMPROVED PHYSICAL AND MENTAL HEALTH

About 25% of the survey sample mentioned improved physical health, and 18% experienced overcoming depression and panic attacks.

Channeling helps with physical, mental, or emotional health issues because we can **go to the origin of the problem**, understand it, and heal it there, at the root. This process may take us to various stories, from early life, our mother's womb, or our soul's origin.

"One of the most powerful benefits is that now, if I start working on a certain issue and I connect to my body, the emotions and thoughts about that subject can make me go instantly to other lives, to the subconscious, liberating and processing the causality link from that starting point which effects in this life. After such a process, external changes are immediate...Many of our body's issues result from unfinished experiences from other lives." (Maria Carmen, Romania)

By connecting deeply with ourselves, we can better manage and **understand our emotional, mental, or behavioral patterns**:

"I have become more conscious of my emotions and can see the bigger picture in situations that arise. I question more about what this situation shows me and how I can grow. It has shown me how to live and love more deeply." (Talaa, Oman)

"Since I started advancing inside me, my journeys for healing emotions, patterns, and situations from the past have brought many revelations, inspiration, guidance, and self-knowledge. This is a process that brings me joy" (Lavinia, Romania)

For some people, such as Maria Carmen or myself, a calling to work with others has opened in time after starting to channel. In this regard, channeling may add new facets and insights to previous healing therapies or open the path to new ones.

"It is amazing how such therapies opened up so profoundly." (Maria Carmen, Romania)

Other people have even found a solution to **dealing with addictions**:

"I no longer suffer under the weight of my past addictions. I can decipher the difference between the voice of my ego and the voice of higher guidance, ultimately leading me toward higher and higher versions of myself. I have a resounding baseline of delight in my life that is unshakable, even in the darker times. I would say consistent practice and the release of layers is important. And lastly, "Trust it is so" When Divine gives you guidance, trust yourself enough to follow it." (Tiffany, Canada)

N. HIGHER, MORE STABLE INCOMES

Abundance is a popular topic in our society and the focus of many spiritual practices, classes and workshops. We often inherit many negative collective beliefs and emotions attached to money that block us from experiencing and enjoying abundance. In channeling, we can **become aware of old mental conditioning and release them**. Thus Hrug, from the United States, mentions an "acquired understanding that abundance is meant for me as well and scarcity is a construct- that came through channeling."

Other answers confirm the same use of channeling in improving our relationship with money and abundance.

"I healed my relationship with money. I understood how I was seeing it, so I changed my perspective. I've started to love it, to feel that I truly deserve it, to call it and keep it in my life "(Mirona, Romania)

The power of materialization or manifestation of our wishes in physical reality is usually closely linked to abundance.

"In less than a month since I started channeling, I bought my dream home that wasn't planned to be bought for at least 2 years. It met all my criteria. It was mind-blowing." (Andreea L., Romania)

For P.C, from Romania, with channeling, "the intention launched in the universe materializes."

"Channeling helps me in manifestation. I feel more connected with my soul." (I.E, Switzerland)

☆ ☆ ☆

10. MAJOR LIFE TRANSFORMATIONS ENABLED BY CHANNELING

When I asked people to name the most important transformation that channeling has brought into their life, most of the answers were linked to experiencing **a direct connection to God** (21%), **increased trust** (14%), **finding the meaning or vocation of their life** (8%) **and releasing old patterns** (8%). Other life-changing experiences are about gaining clarity (6%) and feeling guided (6%), self-discovery and self-development (6%), finding peace (5%), healing (3%), expanded awareness (4%), embracing change (4%), followed by enjoying life, making new choices, experiencing love and forgiveness, safety, magic, freedom, flow, truth or improved relationships.

Everything changes when we embrace what we truly are- manifestations of Divine. These transformations can occur slowly or fast, in the most appropriate way for everyone. Some testimonies speak of very deep and radical life transformations in terms of relationships, abundance, and release of old patterns.

"My life has transformed radically since I started channeling in so many ways that it's hard to formulate a one-page answer. First, I've learned to love myself more and be patient with my growth process, I quit smoking, and my life is way more balanced. Another important thing for me is that I met a partner and am getting married. Last but not least, I moved to another city and love it here." (Calin, Romania)

Veronica from Romania talks about experiencing "a deep transformation of her life: moving from one country to another, I found the place with an opening towards what I need at this moment of my life. Everything becomes orchestrated when you are in alignment with the universe."

Overcoming longtime patterns and stories is also part of these miraculous changes, as underlined by Evangelina from Canada: "I've released all fear around sleeping. I used to have a hard time falling asleep and staying asleep. I would have fears of something bad happening to me while I was asleep, so I had to sleep with a bright light on and ear plugs in. I had night terrors. I channelled and came to peace with my fears, and they have since been released, and I sleep like a baby!! One of the many radical changes."

A. A NEW PERSPECTIVE ON LIFE AND DEATH

The change of perspective regarding life and ourselves is one of the major effects of opening up to the connection with our divinity. We understand that we are part of a bigger orchestration where we each have a role, and things always unfold with a purpose, even if we cannot see it and understand it at that moment. In channeling, we can access a higher, wider perspective on things beyond the expectations and limitations of our minds. We can see the overall image from above, or at least a part that makes more sense for us.

We have a clearer perspective on our place and the role of our actions in the big orchestration of life:

"Channeling has brought clarity in the understanding of the hierarchies in the universe. I understood that we have in us the Divine spark. I received so much love through messages, and I felt so supported. And somehow, from this overflow, I've come to be open to giving love without expecting it back (even if this is exactly what is happening: I receive what I give multiplied by 100. "(Lucia Maria, Romania)

"Now I see how everything is interconnected, and it's easier to make correlations between different moments of my life, what I perceive now, and how things manifest in the physical world.

I learned to ask myself frequently how I feel, what I feel like doing, how beneficial one action is for me compared to others, before making a decision." (Mihaela O., Romania)

"My priorities have rearranged consciously and smoothly, according to what my soul wanted and not necessarily following other people's expectations or social dogma. I enjoy exploring life and seeing every day as a new adventure! I have a much more beautiful relationship with my partner! Working daily with myself, everything around me has changed and reflected my new inner harmony." (C.M., Romania)

With a higher perspective comes **acceptance and trust in the Divine unfolding** of things and the inner guidance of our souls.

Mihaela from Romania talks about experiencing "a higher vision of everything that comes towards me, fulfilment, trust in my strength and Divine."

 "The most important transformation was the change of perspective together with acceptance. Every episode you don't like too much passes easier with softness, acceptance, and the questions: how can I see this thing from another perspective? What did it come to teach me?" (Denisa, Romania)

This acceptance of life just as it is, with its ups and downs that all teach us something about ourselves, leads to expanded awareness, appreciation of life's gifts, and **being more present in our lives**.

"I started to live my life more consciously" (Tanta, Romania)

"My discovery was to accept that everything that comes towards me or us is for our higher good. Nobody wants bad things for us (because Bad doesn't exist). We are here to enjoy this life and learn more things and evolve. The most important part is that when you stop running (towards anything - money, fame, recognition, fulfilment), the magic happens, and you LIVE here and now. I've

LIFE CHANGING EXPERIENCES

Bar chart (% on x-axis, from 0 to 20):

- living in truth
- improved relationships
- being in flow
- freedom
- dealing with emotions
- experiencing magic
- safety
- forgiveness
- love
- making choices
- healing
- embracing change
- expanded awareness
- enjoying life
- peace
- self-development
- guidance
- clarity
- release
- finding life purpose
- trust
- connection

% 0   10   20

acknowledged that everything passes, which is my choice– easier or harder. I have things to learn from everything without agitation and stress. Everything has a meaning! We are love and joy! In channeling meditation, I find peace and reconnect with myself, with the Divine light and wisdom... everything is relaxation and happiness! I love this wonderful state of bliss that I reach. Thank you, thank you, thank you!" (Cristina S., Romania)

Changing the perspective on life and being aware of the Divine orchestration of things naturally leads also to **changing our perspective on death**: this can be seen and accepted as a passage towards a new form of being that doesn't stop the love connection between souls.

"The blessing that channeling has brought into my life was to make peace with the passage to the other plane of my beloved parents! This was the big challenge of my life!" (Kataryna, Romania)

Note. Azrael, also known as the archangel that helps the transition to other planes and the transition of the family left behind in this world, reminds us that life is made of shadow and light, death and rebirth. **Every death is a rebirth for those left behind as well as those who passed away.** Death brings a reconfiguration of those left alive, and new, stronger persons can rise from that grief, if they accept the Divine unfolding. On the other hand, it is important to remember the liberation of those who go beyond the physical realm and its limitations. From this perspective, we may actually come to be happy, at least for them, if not for us yet.

B. BEING IN FLOW

Accepting and embracing life as it is helps us align with the flow of creation. When we quiet the mind and let the soul guide us, we can sense more clearly the most appropriate choices for us in every moment and tune into the most appropriate form and timing for doing what is appropriate for us:

"I understood how many limitations are created by our mind when we are, in fact, much more. And I could let myself be in flow and make the most appropriate choices for me and those around me in every aspect of my life." (Mihaela M., Romania)

We live in a society selling the illusion of speed and action as key factors for achieving success. But in actuality, we cannot hurry the unfolding of things. Everything has its own rhythm, and our body has its own rhythm. We reach a certain place or state only when and if it is appropriate for us to be there. Planning and hurrying are patterns of the mind and the opposite of surrender. Sometimes it may seem that we speed things up, but those things were supposed to be done anyway.

This doesn't mean we don't make plans anymore, only to pay attention to who is planning, as the most appropriate plans come from the heart, not the mind. Our heart knows what is right for us and the perfect rhythm to do it. It knows when to act, when to take a break or continue. In channeling, we can ask what is most appropriate for us to do and when, how, and where to do it. Thus, we align to the perfect Divine flow.

Being in flow also means letting the Divine create whatever is intended to be created through us, not what our ego is planning. Nada, from Oman, says that "I am a Divine vessel and an infinite creative Divine energy flows through me." (Nada, Oman)

The surrender to the Divine flow and orchestration of things forges a **new perspective on changes**. It helps us to embrace them and see the light (i.e., the higher meaning, the soul lessons) even in the most difficult moments:

"I went through some very difficult changes, not catalyzed by me. The surrender, trust, and peace birthed through channeling have helped me embrace the light gifted in these difficulties," says Nadia from Saudi Arabia.

"Even if I experience losses of relationships in my everyday life and I'm not completely pleased with my job, when I connect with Divine, I feel joy, safety, and trust. I feel that everything will be alright, and even if it's not how I want it, I feel like letting the Divine unfold things in their natural way. At that moment, the fight, stress, and sadness disappear, and acceptance comes with trust in Divine. I am delighted that I finally let go of control" (Adriana M., Romania)

Note. Every change is meant to de-create what we were until that moment, what we thought and knew until then. And it forces us to re-create ourselves into a magnificent new being. **Every day, every moment, we recreate ourselves just like a kaleidoscope's beautiful patterns**. And we are infinite kaleidoscopes with infinite images. Our mission here is to discover the infinite ways we can rearrange ourselves, our thoughts, and our beings into magnificence. We came here to experience the most of your divinity in a body and the most of the divinity expressed through other bodies and forms around us.

C. FORGIVENESS

In channeling, we can see and understand events and other persons' behavior from multiple perspectives, being aware of the Divine light at the core of everything and everyone. Thus, we may be able to forgive even the worst, unthinkable actions or words directed towards us because we can identify and understand the lessons behind them and their role in shaping our evolution.

"I've learned to forgive both the persons who hurt me as well as myself" (Sorina, Italy)

"I have learned to forgive myself for anything I have done that I felt ashamed of. I forgave any thoughts or judgments I held against myself or others. I forgave myself for any grief, loss, or feelings of unworthiness." (Ozzy, United Arab Emirates)

When we forgive others, we actually forgive and free ourselves. As creators, we can de-create the links that keep us prisoners in old stories. Forgiveness comes from our heart, that part of ourselves that always knows the truth. The heart knows that we all play specific roles in the various stories of our lives. So, we don't actually forgive the roles, but the souls beyond them, the souls that play a part orchestrated for our growth. We can de-create the pain and its memory through forgiveness, thus stepping forward towards freedom.

D. CONNECTING WITH BEINGS OF LIGHT

The amazing benefit of channeling is that we can safely connect with other beings of light from the infinite, almighty space of Source. Depending on their affinities, people can connect with angels, archangels, ascended masters, galactic consciousness, dragons, unicorns, nature spirits, etc. By doing that, we can understand the various magnificent forms that Divine chooses to manifest in and their role in the tapestry of creation and our life.

In channeling, **we can connect with our higher selves and our light guardians** that help protect, guide, heal, or even teach us.

"I received healing from my guides. I saw past lives and healed misunderstandings and trauma from others that I carried on until now. I acknowledged my potential, and I understood my multiple dimensions. You feel free, whole, present, awakened …you let go of the veils, and you can see higher realms (I call it the White World), energies, and archangels. When you know your Higher Self and your team of angels that are nearby, you understand how protected you are, how much work you need to do, and how much you are loved, and you can turn on this love towards those surrounding you" (Elena C., Romania)

Some of us are meant to **work with such beings of light and introduce them to other people**, to change old mentalities built by various social authorities (i.e., church, books, movies, etc.).

Here are some testimonies from a retreat where I taught people to **connect with the Dragons**:

"I felt a call and followed my intuition. My mind protested a bit, still having some limiting patterns related to dragons, coming from the religious area ... I have to admit that, with all my resistance, some profound transformations took place. I was used to energy therapies, but the dragons' energy was very special. They literally took away the cemented limitations in my liver and the blockage of expression from my throat area in the Vishuddha chakra. Thank you for this chance to be reborn! I felt like sitting on a trampoline above a swimming pool, not knowing if the water would be very cold or hot. And my higher self was whispering to me: "My dear child, you don't know if there is water in the pool or not. But I assure you that as soon as you jump, you will never touch the water, but you will rather discover that you can fly." The most important lesson I learned (I'm still in the process, in fact) is the lesson of letting go of control" (Elena, Germany)

"Flight is a symbol under which my healing journey began, and it seems that this cycle ends with a flight sustained by these forms of energy beyond the highest flight that the mind can perceive on Earth. If I am connected with the spirit of the Eagle very deeply in everything I experience, the perspective of the dragons and the journey they facilitated me with so much support and love only make me connect even stronger in my being, the Divinity and the Earth that is very dear to me. Thanks, everyone!" (Magda, Romania)

"Every day, other Dragons took us to places with big energy portals. They showed me the way and the mission I have to accomplish. I felt their greatness, love for us, and desire to be as close as possible to people. It is incredible how wonderful they are and how many gifts they give us when we open ourselves to them and allow ourselves to receive." (Simona B., Romania)

☆ ☆ ☆

11. TOP 10 CHALLENGES OF CHANNELING

About 70% of the people questioned mentioned a challenge in their channeling experiences.

Most of these challenges are linked to doubt (20.4%) and self-doubt (16%), reaching and maintaining the connection (19.4%), followed far behind by releasing the old (7.5%), opposition from social environment (7.5%), inconsistency of practice (7.5%), the beginning (adjustment) period (7.5%), finding the right of time and context (6.5%), clarity (6.5%) and integration (3.2%).

A. DOUBTING THE PROCESS

The main obstacle to overcome, especially at the beginning of a channeling practice, is the doubt about what comes in channelling and the doubt that we connect with Divine or a specific light being, that they hear and answer our calling. For our mind, it is challenging to trust the intangible and what we were taught to believe as impossible.

As most of the information usually comes in the form of thoughts and ideas, for many people, it is hard to differentiate if the message comes from the mind or higher consciousness.

"It was hard for me to believe I can channel, and it's not my imagination," says Suchitra from Oman.

"In the beginning, it is quite difficult to quiet the mind not to interfere anymore, and to accept, to trust Divine and your intuition" (Cristina S., Romania)

"I have difficulty deciphering between intuition and my thoughts since intuition has grown and become as strong as my thoughts." (Evangelina, Canada)

Solution. The truth is that our mind is a channel. When we connect with Source for example, the mind is connected to a higher vibration, to a universal pool of knowledge. If we record our channeled messages, we can see that what comes in channeling is formulated and explained differently than we would have done in our daily discourse.

So, the way to overcome all this is to simply trust our connection and the messages and see where they take us when we follow that guidance. When we see the results, our confidence grows.

B. REACHING/ MAINTAINING THE CONNECTION

Reaching and maintaining the state of connection may seem difficult, especially in the beginning. The mind is used to roll out all kinds of thoughts that may disturb or sabotage us from feeling the connection. Therefore, people often mention difficulties with **staying focused, overcoming mind agitation or disconnection, or even staying awake during channeling.**

"I experience difficulties in staying focused and staying in the space of the heart instead of the mind space." (Denise, Germany)

Difficulties in **reaching and maintaining the connection or deeply feeling it in the body** can sometimes occur even after a longer practice because the mind is not used to letting go of control: "It happens even now that I cannot disconnect from reality more profoundly (I don't want to lose control), which blocks me from connecting with higher energies." says Narcisa, from Romania.

Solution. You may use deep breathing to bring the focus inside yourself. Thank your mind for all it does for you and ask it to stay quiet in the background, a silent observer and recorder of everything experienced. And even if thoughts occur, it is normal. Just accept them, let them pass, and come back to quiet. Let go of control. Just surrender to whatever comes up for you without analyzing and labelling.

C. SELF-DOUBT

For many people, doubt comes from a lack of trust in their own light and worthiness. That's why self-doubt is a major challenge in connecting with Divine and other light consciousness. Under the influence of many social conditioning, we often perceive ourselves as inferior to others and separated from an almighty, exterior, and frightening God. We've been taught for centuries that we are sinners, and only very few special and pure people can connect with Divine.

That's why, for example, "Am I worthy of all this Love!?" was a question that KS, from Oman, asked herself often in the begging. Now she knows that she is worthy of that Divine love.

Asaad, from the UK, also talks about "learning to trust that I'm connected and learning to receive Divine's love."

Solution. Trust your inner knowing about who you really are: a part of Divine, a part of everything, with your unique place in this world, no matter how insignificant it may seem. Remember that the same energy of Source flows through everything and everyone, including yourself,

TOP 10 CHALLENGES

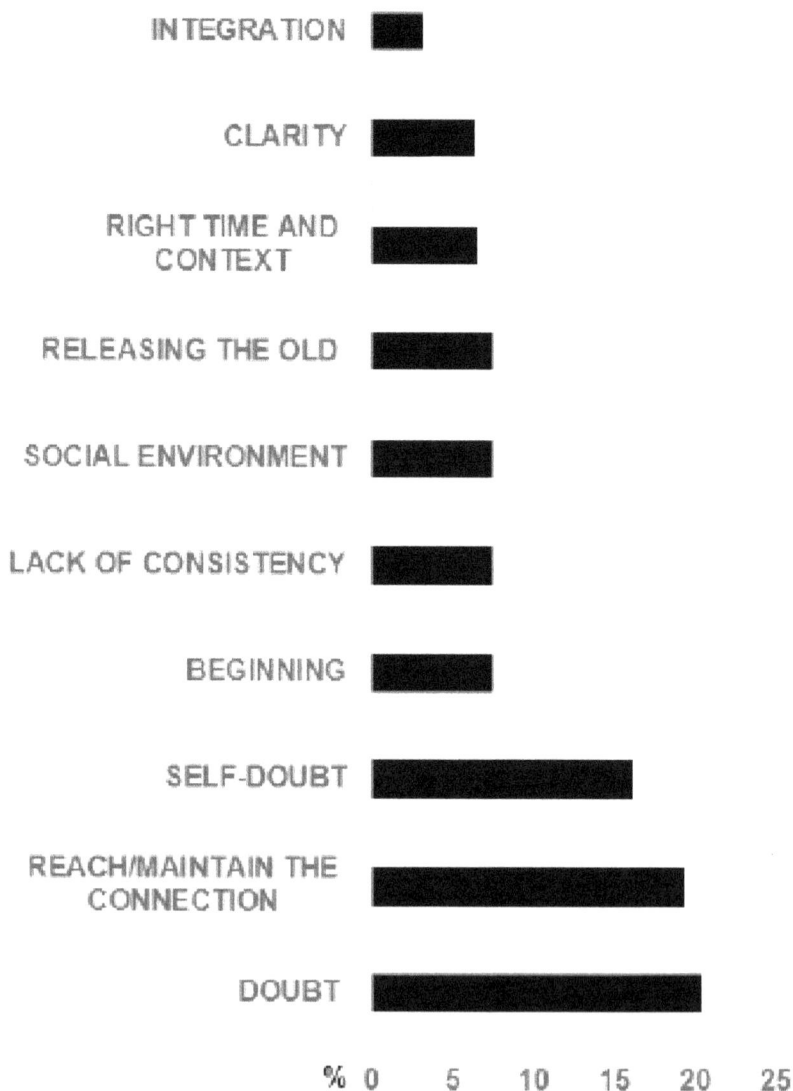

Bar chart showing Top 10 Challenges (% on x-axis from 0 to 25):
- INTEGRATION
- CLARITY
- RIGHT TIME AND CONTEXT
- RELEASING THE OLD
- SOCIAL ENVIRONMENT
- LACK OF CONSISTENCY
- BEGINNING
- SELF-DOUBT
- REACH/MAINTAIN THE CONNECTION
- DOUBT

D. RELEASING THE OLD

Releasing old conditioning (blockages, beliefs, emotional patterns) generates deep inner and outer transformations. Our whole life is practically changing, and this process may sometimes be difficult to experience.

"The process of releasing layers and reprogramming your previously conditioned mind is not an easy one. But over time, it has the power to completely change your life." (Tiffany, Canada)

Fears are part of the old conditioning that limit our connection to Source. The most frequent is the fear of the unknown, of hearing messages we don't want to accept, of not being enough, of not being able to connect, of not receiving any messages, and so on.

Solution. Yes, it's difficult to completely change who you are and the way you live your life. You let go of many layers and identities. The way through that is with acceptance, self-love, and trust in Divine and our soul, trust that everything that happens is for our good.

So, the way to overcome all these fears is through trust and practice. Just enter into channeling, ask for simple, practical answers (don't start with major, life-changing issues), follow them, and when you see their impact, you'll start to trust and let go of the fear.

E. SOCIAL ENVIRONMENT

One of the most frequent external limitations comes from our social environments, such as society in general, cultural context, various authorities (church, school, government), media, friends, family, and partners. They all have different beliefs about Divinity, our relationship with it, or what we can and cannot do in this life.

It's difficult to let go of old beliefs, hence the judgment, rejection, and separation that may sometimes come from those around us who think differently.

To avoid social rejection, punishment, or even losing people from their life, some choose to **hide their practice and beliefs**: "The community I belong to doesn't approve of such practices. I practice with a select few or in secret" (Rasha, Oman).

That's why many people feel the need for a **supporting community** where they can be in their truth, sharing similar interests and values.

"It's hard to find a peer group or a guide. The majority looks sceptically at those who practice channeling like we are crazy," says Violeta from Germany.

Solution. The solution is to do what feels right for you. You don't have to show off, prove something, or convince anybody about your truth. Do what feels right for you, when and where you feel safe, and let your transformation inspire others. Find the appropriate way and timing to explain what you do to the people important in your life so that they have the choice to understand, accept and love as you are. It is not about convincing them of your truth.

At the same time, it is true that the more we advance on our path, some people may disappear from our life as we no longer resonate with them. Those who love and respect us will learn to accept us as we are, even if we think and behave differently. And some will even be inspired by our higher vibration, the balance, and peace in our lives. So, find people who share your values and support each other on your paths.

F. LACK OF CONSISTENCY

If we don't practice, it's not like the connection disappears, but we can't feel its benefits, at least not consciously. It may also reinforce a perception of separation from the practice and Divine (seen as something separate from/in our life).

"I don't give myself enough time to practice. I go to channeling only when I feel somehow misaligned..." (Alexandra P., Romania)

Sometimes it is more comfortable to avoid thinking about it and stay in old patterns.

"It hasn't been something that I have turned to in my grief on a daily basis. It's like eating healthily. We know it is good for us, but we don't do it every day. It's easier to eat the cake." (S.O., Canada)

Solution. The more we connect with the Divine light flowing through us, the more this connection strengthens and clarifies, and it starts to feel like a part of ourselves and our daily life.

G. BEGINNING

The start is usually the most challenging part of all practices. It's a period of uncertainty, of finding your way and adjusting to a reality completely different from what you thought possible a few months or years before. It is about understanding how your channel functions, how you receive messages (mentally, visually, in the body, etc.), and how to interpret them. It is the period where your channel is also opening, sometimes very slowly (softly), other times very fast (or strongly), and your whole being is integrating these processes at various levels in different rhythms. That's why some people experience confusion, doubt, avoidance, not feeling ready, or disappointment because of their unreal expectations or their comparison to others.

"In the beginning, I denied or ignored a lot of the intuition/guidance that I was receiving, and I was leaving it out there until I understood that by following the guidance, I choose to embrace and align with the higher scenario of my life "(Lavinia, Romania)

Solution. Just give yourself time to explore this new tool that you have. Don't put pressure on yourself and let go of expectations. Start practicing and see how it goes for you, see how and what changes from a couple of weeks or months to another, and don't forget to have fun while exploring. Allow yourself to explore, to stumble, to learn from every experience. And don't compare yourself to others because each channel is unique and has its own opening rhythm.

H. THE RIGHT TIME AND CONTEXT

Finding the right context (place and time) for channeling is challenging for some of us. Shutting out the external noise and agitation and finding time for ourselves may seem difficult.

"Sometimes making space for it in my life is a challenge", says Bernie from Oman.

Florina from Romania says, "I don't have time and sometimes neither the right context to practice."

Solution. Find 7-10 minutes daily when you wake up in the morning or late before sleep or whenever you have some alone time during the day (in the car, in nature, or at home). In time, through constant practice, you'll feel so connected to your channel that you will be able to channel in various places and moments, as it is natural because this connection is always there. You can be in channeling when you walk, exercise, dance, cook, clean the house, draw, write, etc.

I. CLARITY

Another challenging aspect is the interpretation of the messages received in channeling, as they are not always straightforward. Some may be symbolic - for example, a color, a symbol, an animal, an image, a feeling in the body, etc.

"There were certain images that my mind didn't understand" (Carmen, Switzerland)

Solution. See what those images or symbols mean for you and what you usually associate them with. As in channeling you receive messages tailored for you, they will come in forms and symbols that we'll make sense only for you. So please don't go and ask people what something means to them. Think about what it means for yourself.

You can also ask some clarification questions in channeling to help you better understand the messages. If no further clarification comes, trust that your channel knows what you are ready to receive at every moment, and if it's something more to know, you will know it in perfect timing. It is also true that sometimes clarifications will come in time when we experience something directly linked to those messages.

J. INTEGRATION

Integrating the experience of the magical worlds beyond the veil with our existence in physical reality is one major challenge. Yet, implementing here the information and activations received from other realms is very important for our balance and well-being.

Hence the questions that Nada, from Oman, has been trying to answer: "How do I step into the reality of this world and integrate with the physical realm after being in such bliss? How can I embody this into my world and my reality? How to embody Divine love and divinity in this world that is fear based?"

Bianca, from Romania, also talks about "keeping the balance with the real world. While the channeling state is something unique, I still needed to accept that I'm in the physical realm, and I needed to find the balance."

Solution. A solution would be to progressively make channeling a part of our life by connecting whenever and wherever we need guidance, by being always aware of our multidimensionality; by letting go of considering this connection something exterior or separate from our day-to-day life; by bringing Divine guidance into every aspect of our physical life: job, family, love life, finances, or various decisions. In time, with trust, opening, and practice, everybody can find their unique way of connecting with Divine and experiencing this connection permanently.

K. OTHER CHALLENGES

Other challenges experienced by people are linked to **temporary blockages** of their channel (that are overcome after acknowledging and releasing the blockage), **physical symptoms** such as fatigue (which can be avoided if we do physical exercise each day when we channel), or **not feeling ready to follow the guidance** that comes in channeling.

☆ ☆ ☆

12. WHERE DO WE GO FROM HERE?

The sky is not the limit in this case, as there is no limit.

Our channel is always open. The Divien talks to us in various forms: through words and images that we see around us, through emotions and sensations in our body, through dreams, music, painting, dance, or through conscious channeling. All these ways highlight our connection with Divine and our multidimensional nature (we exist in multiple planes, and we are the sum of many aspects such as child and adult, physical, emotional, and mental bodies, etc.). It is only up to us to find the best way of connecting with Divine in each moment of our existence. And we find this most appropriate way when we follow our heart.

I know many people who have come to integrate channeling beautifully in various aspects of their life and this has led them to experiencing peace, joy, abundance, and balance. It doesn't mean that channeling makes our life a never-ending joy because existence and evolution in this physical world are mainly made through contrast. Yet, in this regard, channeling helps us to find our way through periods of intense contrast. It helps us to understand the lessons beyond them and to keep at least a spark of peace and balance even when we find ourselves in the eye of the storm. It helps us to feel when we are misaligned and come back easier to alignment. And it allows us to live in truth, our soul's truth.

☆ ☆ ☆

ABOUT THE AUTHOR

My name is **Oana Moon**, and I am a certified channeling practitioner and facilitator. I help people to connect with Source and unveil their inner light.

Channeling is my inner calling and part of my life mission. In the last 4 years, I've come to integrate channeling into my daily life and private practice. Now I help people connect with their own divinity and find their path to self-empowerment and healing.

My journey started with a deep need for belonging and connecting with something bigger beyond physicality. I've always felt like there was something more out there, yet, for a long time, I couldn't find any way in. Therefore, after many years of living in a very mental and competitive environment, my first connection with Source came as the answer to a lifetime search. I've finally come to touch the light and magic I've always felt around me. It seemed like fairy tales coming alive, which was both exciting and scary.

Thus started a profound and amazing journey of uncovering my light, where I've explored various ways of healing and self-development, such as: Dira channeling, the Journey method by Brandon Bays, connecting with angels, dragons, and ascended masters; Ascension classes, Theta Healing, spiritual teaching, and others. I often struggled with doubts and societal conditioning, but the choice to trust my inner guidance led me to things that previously seemed impossible. Offering intuitive readings and weekly group sessions has helped me to build confidence in my channel. In May 2023, I finished 6 Levels (from 7) of Dira Channeling, meaning about 714 days of channeling practice.

You can find me on Facebook (as Oana Moon), Instagram or www.shineinyourlight.com

ALSO BY THE AUTHOR

You may find my children's book about magic on Amazon.

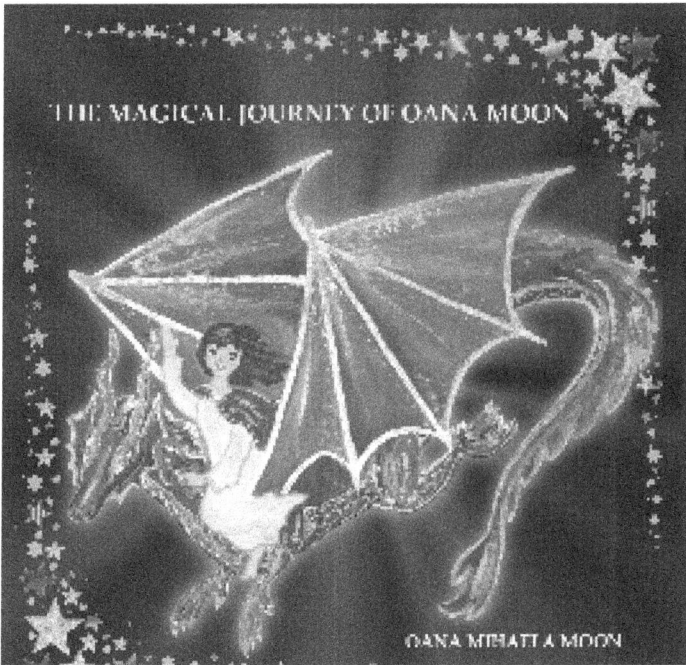

Every day I am grateful to witness how this connection with Source and our inner light changes my life and the lives of people around me

☆ ☆ ☆